To

From

EVERY day GRACE for TEENS

60 DEVOTIONS

Jennifer Gerelds & Denaé Jones

Ellie Claire
Hachette Book Group
1290 Avenue of the Americas, New York, NY 10104
ellieclaire.com

First Edition: February 2019

Ellie Claire is a division of Hachette Book Group, Inc. The Ellie Claire name and
logo are trademarks of Hachette Book Group, Inc.

The publisher is not responsible for websites (or their content) that are not
owned by the publisher.

Scriptures are taken from the following versions: The Holy Bible, New
International Version®, NIV® Copyright © 1973, 1978, 1984, 2011 by Biblica,
Inc.® All rights reserved worldwide. The Holy Bible, New King James Version®
(NKJV). Copyright © 1982 by Thomas Nelson, Inc. The Holy Bible, English
Standard Version® (ESV®), copyright © 2001 by Crossway Bibles, a publishing
ministry of Good News Publishers. The Holy Bible, New Living Translation
(NLT) copyright © 1996, 2004, 2007 by Tyndale House Foundation. Used by
permission of Tyndale House Publishers Inc., Carol Stream, Illinois 60188.
The Message (MSG). Copyright © 1993, 1994, 1995, 1996, 2000, 2001, 2002.
Used by permission of NavPress Publishing Group. Contemporary English
Version® (CEV) Copyright © 1995 American Bible Society. All rights reserved.
New International Reader's Version (NIRV) Copyright © 1995, 1996, 1998, 2014
by Biblica, Inc.®. Used by permission. All rights reserved worldwide. The Holy
Bible, International Children's Bible® (ICB) Copyright© 1986, 1988, 1999,
2015 by Tommy Nelson™, a division of Thomas Nelson. Used by permission.
Third Millennium Bible® (TMB®), New Authorized Version, Copyright © 1998
by Deuel Enterprises, Inc., Gary, SD 57237. All rights reserved.

Interior design and typesetting by Bart Dawson

Library of Congress Cataloging-in-Publication Data has been applied for.

ISBN: 978-1-63326-196-9 (hardcover)

Printed in China

RRD

10 9 8 7 6 5 4 3 2

[God] is looking for people
who will come in simple
dependence upon
His grace, and rest in simple
faith upon His greatness.
At this very moment,
He's looking at you.

JACK HAYFORD

CONTENTS

INTRODUCTIONS

During most of my growing-up years, I understood that faith in Jesus saved me (simple enough), but I felt like it was up to me to stay in God's good graces—as well as everyone else's. I tried so hard to please God, my parents, my teachers, and my friends by doing everything right. I feared failure so much, mainly because I thought that if I failed, I would lose the admiration and affection of everyone I loved, including God.

Decades later, after a long series of devastating circumstances, Jesus showed me why my efforts would never be enough, why I could—and should—stop trying so hard to be loved and accepted: *I already was.*

And so are you. Jesus has already done what we could never do—and that was live a perfect life. His sacrifice on the cross earned our freedom to live forever as God's fully loved children, simply by trusting Him. It really is amazing grace.

We hope that as you read *Everyday Grace for Teens*, you get a tiny glimpse each day of God's great acceptance of and affection for you—and the life-changing power His love brings. You matter so much to God and were created to make a difference. Let the truth of God's Word and the light of His presence lead you there.

—Jennifer Gerelds

Before we started this book, we asked teens how they have experienced God's grace. Each gave examples of how grace truly is amazing! However, it often came on the heels of brokenness and messiness in their lives. They wanted to know how God shows up in the middle of it.

Yes, sometimes grace can be a heavy topic, but it's awesome knowing we are forgiven and there is nothing we can do to make God stop loving us! He's cool like that.

We hope you enjoy our stories of God's amazing grace. As you read each devotion, take a few moments to reflect on how you have experienced grace in your life and through your story. Drink in His grace until you are so full it overflows to all those around you.

—Denaé Jones

AMAZING YOU!

*For I am convinced that neither death nor life,
neither angels nor demons, neither the present
nor the future, nor any powers,
neither height nor depth, nor anything else
in all creation, will be able to separate us
from the love of God
that is in Christ Jesus our Lord.*

ROMANS 8:38–39 NIV

You are beautiful beyond your outward beauty.
You are smarter than just what you learn in
school.
You have talent that is still untapped.
You have ideas that are uniquely yours.
Your heart is full of love and compassion.
Your dreams are reachable.
Your bank account doesn't matter, because
your worth is immeasurable!
You are loved more than you can possibly
comprehend.
You, my dear friend, are breathtaking!

You might be thinking that I've never met you, so how could I know this? Easy! I know your Creator. He created you to be unlike anyone else. He put you here in this exact place, at this exact moment in history, for a reason. He has incredible plans for your life, far beyond what you've probably imagined. Your talent, your compassion, your heart can be used to make this world a better place because you are in it. Being a child of God is so incredible! *DJ*

. . . .

Father God, thank You for Your heavenly
fingerprint on my life!
Help me not take one single gift for granted.

No one else can live our story.
This is our time to shine!
Get rid of the question marks and
replace them with explanation points!

LISA BEVERE

BY DESIGN

They know the truth about God because he has made it obvious to them. For ever since the world was created, people have seen the earth and sky. Through everything God made, they can clearly see his invisible qualities— his eternal power and divine nature.

ROMANS 1:19–20 NLT

Right now, your hands are holding this book, and your eyes are seeing this page. Your brain is at work, deciphering meaning—even while your heart is pumping and your lungs are breathing. Take one look outside your window and you'll see that every part, from the earth below to the sky above, operates so differently and yet simultaneously and succinctly—a complex and unified system that shouts a message we don't want to miss: Intricate designs like us—like the world—have a designer.

For instance, the phone (probably within hand's reach) didn't become *smart* by itself. The fridge didn't simply appear as a stroke of good fortune. Intelligent people thought them up, built them, and brought them into our lives intentionally.

In the same way, the entire universe around us also operates with planned purpose. Every shining star, every painted sunset, every microscopic miracle is a visible invitation to get to know the incredible God who made and sustains it all. He put us on *this* planet at *this* time in history for one mind-blowing reason: to worship Him by enjoying Him and His family forever. Life is simply one cosmic-sized love story between God and His people. *JG*

. . . .

God, thank You for this world
and the ways You show Yourself in it.
Help me to know You more!

God has a wonderful plan for each person
He has chosen. He knew even before
He created this world what beauty
He would bring forth from our lives.

LOUISE B. WYLY

PAID IN FULL

*But he said to me, "My grace is sufficient for you,
for my power is made perfect in weakness."*

2 CORINTHIANS 12:9 NIV

Imagine choosing the perfect gift for the person you love most. You wait with great anticipation for them to receive it!

Your gift is delivered, but day after day, it sits unopened. They want to open it, but get too busy. They wonder if they need a gift in return. Some of their friends laugh at it. Feeling as if they don't deserve it, they pick up the package to throw it away. For the first time, they see your note on the bottom. It says, "I love you. I forgive you." The box is stamped *'Paid in full.'* Finally, they understand.

That's a glimpse of grace. Jesus gave us His perfect gift on the cross, even when we didn't deserve it. His life was the ultimate sacrifice for our sins. Some of us have faith and rejoice that we are forgiven! Some mock Him. Some won't even accept Him. But He loves each and every one of us so much! Yes, even in our sinfulness.

Through faith, God's grace is given to us, and our debt is paid in full. *DJ*

• • • • • • • • • •

Jesus, thank You for loving us
enough to die for our sins.
Help me never to take Your gift for granted!

Each day is a treasure box of gifts from God,
just waiting to be opened.
Open your gifts with excitement!
You will find forgiveness
attached to ribbons of joy.
You will find love wrapped in sparkling gems.

JOAN CLAYTON

MORNING MIRACLES

*And let us consider how we may spur one another
on toward love and good deeds, not giving up meeting
together, as some are in the habit of doing,
but encouraging one another—and all the more
as you see the Day approaching.*

HEBREWS 10:24–25 NIV

U uuuuuugggghhhhh," she groaned as her body remained curled in the fetal position under her covers.

"I have to get up every morning for school," she moaned. "Whyyy can't we just sleep on Sunday?" She stalled. I started to answer in our usual early morning wake-up argument ritual when it struck me. *What would happen if our own body parts revolted that way?* Like, what if one morning we woke up and our eyes just said, "Nope, not today. We've been looking around all week and today we're taking a break?"

At times, gathering together with other believers for church may feel outdated or unnecessary. Certainly, a million other options vie for that time. But we don't want to miss out on the magnificent work God is building around the world! Church isn't a structure, it's His Spirit working with power inside each of His kids, using our unique gifts to bring it all together as one body. When we come together to worship and serve, spectacular miracles happen, souls get saved, and we experience God in ways we'd never find by staying asleep. *JG*

* * * * * * * * * *

Jesus, give me strength to get up
when I'm feeling lazy and look for ways
to build up Your body.

I spent twenty years of my life trying
to recruit people out of local churches
and into missions structures so that they
could be involved in fulfilling
God's global mission. Now I have another idea.
Let's take God's global mission and put it
right in the middle of the local church!

GEORGE MILEY

A DO-OVER

Could it be any clearer?
Our old way of life was nailed
to the cross with Christ,
a decisive end to that sin-miserable life.

ROMANS 6:6 TMB

Sometimes we feel like we have gone past the point of forgiveness. Certain parts of our past are so ugly. We can't escape the guilt we feel from bad choices we made. We are embarrassed to admit how we have hurt others. Sometimes we can't even forgive ourselves. How could God possibly forgive us? How can He love us through all of our sinfulness?

Here's the thing: Nothing we do can make God stop loving us. Nothing! Jesus didn't die on the cross for just a couple of our sins. He died for all of them. Jesus was perfect because He knew we couldn't be. Through His ultimate sacrifice, we got the gift of grace, which is God's unconditional love. He's not sitting with His arms crossed in disappointment. He's giving us a wink. He's putting a hand on our shoulder and saying, "Put your faith in Me. You'll get it right next time."

It's never too late for a do-over. *DJ*

• • • • • • • • • •

Jesus, thank You for Your sacrifice,
once and for all.
Forgive me for all the times
I have sinned against You.

There was a time I was not following God.
In fact, I was doing everything I could
to ignore His voice. My God, though,
He is the God of *It's never too late.*
The word He spoke to me is *still.*
I still love you. I am still going to use you.
I still have some beautiful plans for you.
You still have the power of Jesus Christ within you.
You are still worthy. I am still going to pursue you.
That's my God!

CHLOE STAM

FIRED UP

And now, Israel, what does the L<small>ORD</small> your God ask of you but to fear the L<small>ORD</small> your God, to walk in obedience to him, to love him, to serve the L<small>ORD</small> your God with all your heart and with all your soul, and to observe the L<small>ORD</small>'s commands and decrees that I am giving you today for your own good?

DEUTERONOMY 10:12–13 NIV

I am not a fan of winter, but I love to challenge the season's cold with a good fire pit, chairs, and people circled around to soak in the smoky warmth, making s'mores and some good conversation. It's almost magical watching the orange and amber flames dance against a dark night sky. But while the fire is both mesmerizing and mysterious, I'm not fooled. Fire is lovely in my fire pit, but ferocious when it rages over land and homes.

My experience with fire helps me understand something else I enjoy but can never contain. While I'm comforted by the warmth of God's grace and love, I can't lose sight of His fearful holiness and power. Without Christ's covering, we would all be completely consumed! The reality of His righteous authority keeps me in my proper place: worshipping in awe and wonder at this incredible God who could choose to end me right now, but instead comforts me and draws me close with an everlasting love. *JG*

· · · · · · · · · ·

Today, come closer to Your Father, and feel
the power of His grace and love for You.
Jesus, shield me from what my sins
deserve and free me to experience
God's incredible goodness and glory.

It is God's all-consuming love that fuels us
to invite others to experience His grace.
The world around us needs to feel
the warmth of our Father's love, too!

SOCIAL CONFINEMENT

So then faith comes by hearing,
and hearing by the word of God.

ROMANS 10:17 NKJV

I heard a sixteen-year-old girl say she wished cell phones were never invented. She was tired of how it held her captive. If she didn't answer a text right away, people got worried. If she didn't keep up the streaks on Snapchat, friends gave her a hard time. If she didn't "friend" someone, they got upset.

Our phones are our computer, camera, social connection, gaming and guidance system. That's not necessarily a bad thing as long as we use it in moderation and keep our intentions in check.

Are we posting selfies because there is a great story to tell, or just to fish for compliments? Did we post that comment to lift someone up, or put them down? Are we spending more time scrolling through everyone else's posed, filtered, highlight reel on social media than we are living our own life? Are we letting our worth and value be determined by other people's comments?

Consider this: Isn't what God thinks of our actions more important than what other people think of us? Are there any changes we need to make? *DJ*

· · · · · · · · · ·

Father, help me to take time to unplug
from the world and plug in to the real power source—
Your Word in Holy Scripture.

Sooner or later we all discover that the important
moments in life are not the advertised ones,
not the birthdays, the graduations,
the weddings, not the great goals achieved.
The real milestones are less prepossessing.
They come to the door of memory.

SUSAN B. ANTHONY

FAMILY FIGHTS

*All praise to God, the Father of our Lord Jesus Christ.
God is our merciful Father and the source of all comfort.
He comforts us in all our troubles so that we can
comfort others. When they are troubled, we will be able
to give them the same comfort God has given us.
For the more we suffer for Christ, the more God will
shower us with his comfort through Christ.*

2 CORINTHIANS 1:3–5 NLT

She had asked to go on the church retreat because she wanted to make some new friends. Instead, my daughter experienced utter rejection. It appeared that when the main speaker invited kids to write down their honest questions about God on the chalkboard up front, her kind of wondering was just too real. Kids reacted by writing hateful words beside her query, condemning her for having even asked.

It's no wonder my daughter spent the next several years hating church and the people in it. It hurts when anyone wounds us, but especially when the pain comes from people claiming to be Christians. The hypocrisy can make us want to walk away from it all.

But instead of giving up on God's family—who are just forgiven sinners just like us—what if we go to God with our pain instead? What if we allowed those wounds to sharpen our wonder of all that Jesus endured and forgave for us? When we seek comfort in God's consistent care, He not only heals us with His unfailing love, but He also shapes our hearts in the process. We become safer places for other hurting people to find comfort and hope when they need it most. *JG*

. . . .

Jesus, fill me with Your compassion
and help me comfort those
who've been hurt by others.

Compassion costs. It is easy enough to argue, criticize and condemn, but redemption is costly, and comfort draws from the deep. Brains can argue, but it takes heart to comfort.

SAMUEL CHADWICK

Grace means there is nothing
I can do to make God love me
more, and nothing I can
do to make God love me less.
It means that I, even I who
deserve the opposite, am invited
to take my place at the table
in God's family.

PHILIP YANCEY

PRESSURE RELEASE BUTTON

If you are tired from carrying heavy burdens,
come to me and I will give you rest.
Take the yoke I give you. Put it on your shoulders
and learn from me. I am gentle and humble,
and you will find rest. This yoke is easy to bear,
and this burden is light.

MATTHEW 11:28–30 CEV

Just sitting in class, you can feel your stomach twisting into knots. *How am I ever going to get everything done?* The stress tsunami building in your mind has already unleashed waves of panic before your project even starts. What if you drown under the pressure?

Thank God Jesus offers an awesome escape route. It's found in His presence. We just come to Him right where we are through prayer, and He promises to lighten our load. But how does it work, when you're staring at a real deadline?

Jesus says our work is super easy. *Just come to Me.* Simply put, God always keeps His promises. And He has promised to protect you and direct your steps when you seek His help and guidance first. It doesn't mean you'll ace every test, or that you'll avoid failure every time. But as you do your very best, God will move mountains to make your path straight. When we truly believe God's got our back, we'll rest in His peace as He leads us through life's valleys and peaks to places greater than we ever could have planned on our own. *JG*

• • • • • • • • • •

Lord, I believe—help my unbelief!
Please fill me with Your peace
as I trust You to lead my life.

Either sin is with you, lying on your shoulders,
or it is lying on Christ, the Lamb of God.
Now if it is lying on your back, you are lost;
but if it is resting on Christ, you are free,
and you will be saved.
Now choose what you want.

MARTIN LUTHER

VISIBLE

She gave this name to the Lord who spoke to her:
"You are the God who sees me," for she said,
"I have now seen the One who sees me."

GENESIS 16:13–14 NIV

Have you ever felt overlooked? Maybe you've had a great school year and are still not recognized at the awards ceremony. Maybe you worked extra hard at your job, only to have someone else take the credit. Maybe you've gone above and beyond at home or in your community, and realize that it is a thankless job.

We feel so unappreciated in moments like that, but I encourage you to keep being awesome anyway! Your extra effort, your hard work, and even your mistakes are shaping you into the person God wants you to be.

Above all else, know that even though others may not recognize your efforts, God does. One of the names of God in the Hebrew Bible is *El Roi*, which means "the God who sees." In Matthew 6 of the Bible, we read about how we can pray, fast, and give to others without anyone knowing. However "the Father, who sees what is done in secret, will reward you" (verse 4). How great is that! As it turns out, random acts of kindness have always been cool. *DJ*

•   •   •   •   •   •   •   •   •   •

Father, it makes me happy to know
I make You happy!
Thank You for love and laughter.

Go out of your way to be as kind as possible.

JULIA BOWEN

Carry out a random act of kindness
with no expectation of reward,
safe in the knowledge that one day,
someone might do the same for you.

PRINCESS DIANA OF WALES

PERFECT POWER

*Three times I pleaded with the Lord to take it away
from me. But he said to me, "My grace is sufficient
for you, for my power is made perfect in weakness."
Therefore I will boast all the more gladly about
my weaknesses, so that Christ's power may rest on me.*

2 CORINTHIANS 12:8–9 NIV

As she sat alone at the table in the lunchroom, she couldn't stop the tears—or the questions reverberating through her mind: *Why would You do this, God? I don't like the way You made me!*

Diagnosed with high-functioning autism years ago, she had spent her young life struggling to make friends and make sense out of a world that often overlooked the incredible creativity and ingenuity her way of thinking brought to it. She wished it would go away so she could be like everyone else.

But fast-forward five years, and she began to see the wisdom in God's plan. Because of her quirky interests that used to seem so strange, she now stood apart as an expert in her field. God had turned the very facets of her personality that she felt were her greatest weakness into exactly what the world around her needed.

It's just how God always works. In His divine wisdom, He never makes mistakes. Though we may question why He chose to craft our bodies and minds the way He did, we can relax knowing that God's thoughts are higher—and way better—than ours. If we choose to trust Him and what He's doing through us, we will see God work His glory through us in the most unpredictable, unimaginable, and awesome ways ever.

What are your weaknesses you have wished away in the past? Will you believe that God, in His goodness, plans to show His glory through those struggles? *JG*

• • • • • • • • • •

God, thank You for my problems.
I'm trusting You to use them in my life
for Your glory and to make me stronger.

But God chose the foolish things of the world to shame the wise; God chose the weak things of the world to shame the strong.

1 CORINTHIANS 1:27 NIV

CALLED BY NAME

Do not be afraid, for I have ransomed you.
I have called you by name; you are mine.

ISAIAH 43:1 NLT

When I was six years old, I caught a turtle in our field and named him Hemorrhoid. Of course, I had no idea what a hemorrhoid was. I had just heard the word and thought it would be a fine name for my turtle. I didn't understand *why* my mom kept insisting that I think of something more suitable.

Although the name I chose for that poor creature was unfortunate, I knew that giving a name was important. It bestowed a sense of importance and labeled it as my own.

The Bible tells us that God has called each of us by name. Not just by our given names, however. He claims us as His own in a lot of different ways. He says we are His children, His friends, a branch of the true vine, His heirs, saints, His chosen, His workmanship, a member of His body, and a citizen of heaven, just to name a few! Luke 12:7

tells us that the very hairs on our head are numbered. How much God must love us to take such care! *DJ*

• • • • • • • • • •

Thank You, Father God, for Your names
in Scripture that reveal who You are:
Aba, Elohim, El Shaddai, Yahweh,
Jehovah, Adonai!
Thank You for loving us so!

God is every moment totally aware
of each one of us. Totally aware in intense
concentration and love....
No one passes through any area of life, happy
or tragic, without the attention of God.

EUGENIA PRICE

LOOKING FOR LIKES

Just thinking of my troubles and my lonely wandering makes me miserable. That's all I ever think about, and I am depressed. Then I remember something that fills me with hope. The LORD's kindness never fails!

LAMENTATIONS 3:19–22 CEV

Flipping through her Instagram feed, she couldn't help but feel left out. It seemed like everyone else was having the time of their lives, and looking great while doing it. She, however, was at home, on her bed, on her phone—as usual. At least she knew how to fake it, as she swapped apps and Snapchatted her signature duck face and peace sign. *No one else has to know how alone I feel*, she decided. She knew if she kept herself distracted enough, it could numb her sadness, for a little while at least.

Truth be told, we all go to great lengths to ward off loneliness. We find context and connection through community, and it's no wonder we find ourselves tied to what everyone else says and does. Yet no number of likes ever satisfies our soul's search for real relationship.

But we have a resource who does! God invites us through our loneliness to look beyond the world we see to where He is waiting to talk with us. Unlike superficial posts, Jesus sees our hearts, and He not only loves us for who we are right now, but He sees our future potential and likes us for all of eternity! *JG*

. . . .

*Jesus, help me use my loneliness
as a reminder to spend time with You.
Thank You for liking me!*

God knows the rhythm of my spirit
and my heart thoughts.
He is as close as breathing.

HOLDING GRUDGES

Therefore, there is now no condemnation for those who are in Christ Jesus, because through Christ Jesus the law of the Spirit who gives life has set you free from the law of sin and death.

ROMANS 8:1–2 NIV

I don't know about you, but there have been times when I have felt so badly about something I've done that, even after I've truly repented, I keep confessing the same sin. Sometimes I think of God in a human sense. Like, I know I said I'm sorry, but I'm positive He's still disappointed in me. And since He doesn't seem to be punishing me, I get busy trying to punish myself with constant reminders of the guilt and shame.

That is not how God wants us to behave. In fact, once we have confessed our sin, it's the exact opposite. The Bible tells us in Psalm 103:11–12 that God's love for us is so great that He casts our sins as far as the east is from the west. God is not human. He doesn't hold a grudge.

Is there anyone you are holding a grudge against? Is there anyone holding a grudge against you? What steps could you take today to build a bridge of forgiveness? *DJ*

• • • • • • • • • •

*Lord, thank You for forgiving my sins
the first time. Help me to do the same
when others sin against me.*

Holding a grudge doesn't make you strong.
It makes you bitter.

DAVE WILLIS

Regardless of our past, something confessed
is something forgotten. It's so nice to go to bed
at night knowing that God doesn't keep tabs!

JENNIFER THOMAS

FOUL PLAY

How far has the LORD taken our sins from us?
Farther than the distance from east to west!

PSALM 103:12 CEV

She got her first whiff in second period as she leaned over to get her history book out of her backpack. *What is that?* she wondered at the strangely sour smell. In the hall, it happened again. As students walked by, the scent seemed to haunt her. But by fourth period, she saw the source as she unzipped her bag—that telltale stain on the fabric's seam. *Oh no.* She held it up to her nose.

Are you kidding me! she exhaled in a horrified whisper. Rooskin, her beloved Maltese, had done a dastardly deed. And she had been carrying the stench around all day!

Even if your dog is potty trained, we all know what it's like carrying the stench of some secret sin on our backs. We might not recognize the source, but we can smell the bad attitude—the bitterness, rebellion, jealousy, etc.—a mile away. The great news is that God knows the source of our issue and how to get rid of it. Just admit your situation, and hand the garbage over to God. He'll toss it as far away from you as the east is from the west, never to return. *JG*

•   •   •   •   •   •   •   •   •   •

*Jesus, thank You for taking away
the unbearable stench of my sins forever!*

"I must be dreaming," he thought;
but although he stood still for a few minutes,
and rubbed his eyes, the burden did not
come back...the King had really taken
the weight from his shoulders forever.

HELEN L. TAYLOR

AM I SAVED?

If you declare with your mouth, "Jesus is Lord," and believe in your heart that God raised him from the dead, you will be saved. For it is with your heart that you believe and are justified, and it is with your mouth that you profess your faith and are saved.

ROMANS 10:9–10 NIV

A mom got the call that is every parent's nightmare. Her son had been in an accident. He had died and been brought back several times, and now was hanging in the balance between life and death.

She was terrified of what might be lost. Then she looked down at the Bible in her hand, and asked herself an important question: *Do I really believe this or not?* If the answer is yes, we can't lose. If he lives, we win. If he dies, and Jesus welcomes him into heaven, we still win. Her spirit was at peace, because she knew God's truth and our salvation through His grace.

Have you humbled yourself before God, and asked Him to live within you? Have you confessed your sins and try to live the way God wants you to live? If so, your spirit can be at peace as well. Why wait? *DJ*

• • • • • • • • • •

Dear Jesus, thank You for dying on the cross
for the forgiveness of my sins.
I give my life to You.

For all its peculiarities and unevenness,
the Bible has a simple story. God made man.
Man rejected God. God won't give up until
He wins him back. If there are a thousand steps
between us and Him, He will take all but one.
But He will leave the final one for us.
The choice is ours.

MAX LUCADO

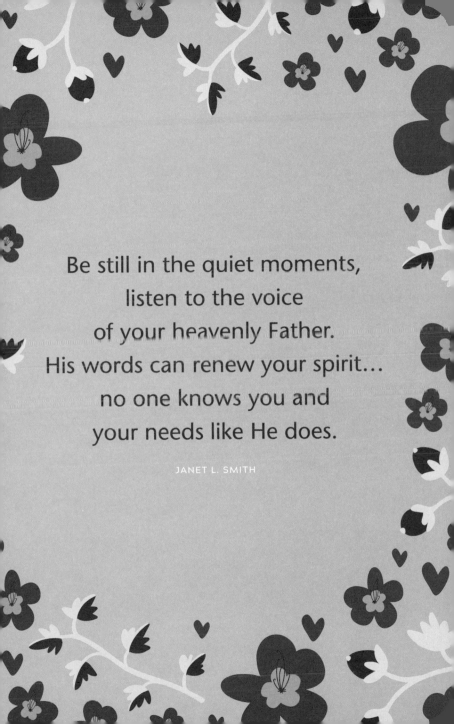

Be still in the quiet moments,
listen to the voice
of your heavenly Father.
His words can renew your spirit…
no one knows you and
your needs like He does.

JANET L. SMITH

MOLDING MINDS

The tools of our trade aren't for marketing or manipulation, but they are for demolishing that entire massively corrupt culture. We use our powerful God-tools for smashing warped philosophies, tearing down barriers erected against the truth of God, fitting every loose thought and emotion and impulse into the structure of life shaped by Christ.

2 CORINTHIANS 10:5–6 MSG

As the potter's wheel spun, she pressed her thumb in the center, rounding out the lump of clay. Slowly a bowl took shape, thinning and stretching as her fingers pressed in from outside. She was pleased, until her creation suddenly took a wrong turn. Warped and wobbling, the pot weakened under excess water. So she scrapped her creation, strengthened her clay, and began the process again.

Like clay on a wheel, every day our minds are spinning with thoughts and ideas, our lives pressed into shape by what we believe. When God's written Word forms our foundation, we grow into strong vessels filled with His presence and purpose. But if we water our lives down with the world's way of thinking, our perspective of God warps and our lives bend grossly out of shape.

Whenever your thoughts stray from God's truth, scrap that line of thinking and start over. Search the Scriptures for what God says is true and press in to apply it. When we do, a beautiful mind takes shape, molding the rest of our lives with truth and grace. *JG*

• • • • • • • • • •

Lord, please help me to notice
warped thinking and give me the power
to start over with Your truth.

Finally, brothers, whatever is true, whatever is honorable, whatever is just, whatever is pure, whatever is lovely, whatever is commendable, if there is any excellence, if there is anything worthy of praise, think about these things.

PHILIPPIANS 4:8 ESV

FEAR OF MISSING OUT

*Don't copy the behavior and customs of this world,
but let God transform you into a new person
by changing the way you think. Then you will learn
to know God's will for you, which is good
and pleasing and perfect.*

ROMANS 12:2 NLT

We've probably all overheard a conversation about some great party, and it sounds like everyone attended but us. Or maybe we scrolled through social media and saw a picture of our friends having a great time, and we weren't included.

Nobody wants to feel left out, and sometimes it can be hurtful. In fact, it's easy to get a bit jealous when we feel like friends are bonding without us. What would it look like if, instead of letting jealousy take hold, we paused to take our feelings of rejection to God and pray for our friends?

God multiplies our love. He gives us the capacity to bond with more than just one person at a time. Each person fills our lives in different ways. We might go to one person for help with schoolwork, another to share a hobby, and another to talk about faith. Rest assured that you are that person to someone as well! *DJ*

. . . .

Lord, thank You for my friends!
Give me discernment to know when
to join in and when to step back. And help me
to come to You when I am feeling left out.

I met my best friend when she was
the new girl at school and I stepped in as kids
were picking on her. Then she stuck up for me
when I was being bullied. Every day since then,
I've looked for people who seem lonely or need
help, and I go over and talk to them.
I know what it's like to be left out,
so I want to be that friend to someone else.

PAIGE JONES

HOLDING HANDS

So do not fear, for I am with you; do not be dismayed,
for I am your God. I will strengthen you and help you;
I will uphold you with my righteous right hand.

ISAIAH 41:10 NIV

When we were kids, we found comfort holding Mom or Dad's hand whenever we walked places. With them by our side, we were free to explore this great big world without any fear.

But we're older now, and wiser to how the real world works. Parts of it are still wonderful, but worry now clouds some of the landscape—especially when we watch the news. Life looks less like a playground and more like a potential minefield as the pressures from school, parents, and growing up begin to mount. How will we ever feel safe going outside? How do we ward off the depression and anxiety that brings so many people down?

We remember that we don't walk alone. We simply look up and slip our hand into the One who holds this world. Though the terrain gets treacherous at times, God is *never* going to let us go. We can walk through a scary world in perfect peace because our God promises to never leave our side, and He works out all that we encounter for our good as we trust Him. *JG*

. . . .

Jesus, how can I ever be afraid
when I know You're right here with me?
I believe Your promise!

In peace I will lie down and sleep,
for you alone, LORD, make me dwell in safety.

PSALM 4.8 NIV

When I am with God my fear is gone;
in the great quiet of God my troubles
are as the pebbles on the road,
my joys are like the everlasting hills.

WALTER RAUSCHENBUSCH

THE TRUE YOU

*For by one sacrifice he has made perfect forever
those who are being made holy.*

HEBREWS 10:14 NIV

My mom sent me a pink gorilla singing telegram to school during my lunch with upperclassmen on my sixteen birthday. It handed me bananas and a balloon and put a hat on my head. I was mortified! I feared I would be the laughingstock of the school! And I was. For a minute. I lived through it and rebounded quickly because, frankly, everyone was glad it was me and not them!

Sometimes we're afraid people will like us less if they see our flaws, but you know what? Everyone has them! Even the people who criticize you for yours. Just remember that anyone can criticize and judge. It takes a grace-filled person not to take it personally and resist doing the same thing to others.

You were given gifts, talents, and maybe even flaws for a reason. Maybe they are quirky, but that's okay! God put you here, at this moment in time, because this world needs you just the way you are. If we look different, or come from a different background, or have different abilities, there is no shame in that. In fact, God loves variety. He made it that way! *DJ*

. . . .

Father, help me embrace my uniqueness!
Help me not to point out the flaws in others.

Sometimes I feel like I was supposed to be born
in a different generation, but I know God
put me here when He did for a reason.
It's fun to keep figuring out what His reason is!

CARA BOWEN

If you depend on God's grace,
there is no such thing as impossible.

SRI CHINMOY

THE PRAYER APP

*The prayer of a righteous person
is powerful and effective.*

JAMES 5:16 NIV

Older people wake up and turn on the news. We, however, simply touch the screen and a million Snapchats we missed during the night light up our phones, the notifications seeming to never end. It isn't easy staying in the know, either. Streaks must be kept, and cool new shots constantly conceived and sent—at just the right time. There's a strategy to it all, and if we're completely honest, it's an exhausting endeavor, almost 24/7.

But there is an old-school way that outperforms any app in keeping us connected with what really matters. And we don't even have to unlock it with a fingerprint. Prayer, the simple act of talking and listening to God, unpacks a supernatural strength for all we're facing in our day.

Let's be real. No amount of texting or talking, framing or fuming will alter the amount of drama that girl in your class dishes out. And wishing and working schemes won't make that cute boy love you—or even like your pics. But in prayer, we can bring every problem to God, who has the power to move in ways we can't even imagine. Unlike all our electronic distractions that eat up our time with nothing to really show for it, time spent with God makes a real impact on everyone we lift up. He hears our cries and answers every time we call. Reliable and faithful to the core, our God acts when His people pray, and He promises to work out every issue in our best interest. *JG*

• • • • • • • • • •

God, I'm amazed that You not only listen to me,
but You answer when I pray. Thank You!!

Praying unlocks the doors of heaven and releases
the power of God… Whether prayer changes
our situation or not, one thing is certain:
Prayer will change us!

BILLY GRAHAM

ENVY

For where you have envy and selfish ambition,
there you find disorder and every evil practice.

JAMES 3:16 NIV

My best friend and I have known each other since kindergarten. We played the same sports, had the same friends, went to the same places, and shared the same secrets. There were rough patches, though. Especially when we were in sixth grade and started really paying attention to boys paying attention to us. I realized that every boy I liked, liked her. I don't remember rallying the troops, but when I got mad at her, all of our mutual friends did too. For weeks, they called her names and left her out. I'm embarrassed to say that I allowed it to happen, because people were finally paying attention to me.

Luckily, my friend, who had always been loving and supportive toward me, reached out once again and extended grace. She didn't have to forgive me, but she did. I am so thankful, because it changed my heart, and opened my eyes to how much damage envy could cause.

It made our friendship stronger than ever, and we have been inseparable ever since.

Are you holding on to envy? If so, turn it over to our Lord today. *DJ*

. . . .

*Dear heavenly Father, please
guard my heart and bring down walls
that have been built by envy.*

Do you know that nothing you do in this life
will ever matter, unless it is about loving God
and loving the people He has made?

FRANCIS CHAN

NAMED

*The nations will see your vindication, and all kings
your glory; you will be called by a new name that
the mouth of the L*ORD *will bestow. You will be
a crown of splendor in the L*ORD*'s hand,
a royal diadem in the hand of your God.*

ISAIAH 62:2–3 NIV

She laughed it off. She always did, whenever her friends would joke about how "wild" she was the weekend before. After all, she had an image to uphold—though the façade was killing her.

For as long as she could remember, she felt like a failure. At first, it was just from mistakes she made. But over time, in her mind it became who she was. "I'm just *that* girl," she told herself. Guilt and shame drowned the person she dreamed she'd be. Now she just found it better to pretend she wanted it that way.

That's how shame always works. It sabotages our hope and tries to tell us we are worthless. Our enemy, the devil, loves to shove our guilt and failures in our face whenever we try to turn a different direction. But, child of God, don't let it. Your Savior died in your place so that you wear a new name: His. And no weapon or accusation formed against you will stand.

Failures no longer define us. Instead, God uses them to refine our character when we simply repent. God frees us to be real as we rest in who He is and who He says we are. *JG*

• • • • • • • • • •

God, thank You for declaring me perfect
in Your sight through the blood of Jesus.
What amazing grace!

"Any accuser who takes you to court will be dismissed as a liar. This is what God's servants can expect. I'll see to it that everything works out for the best." God's Decree.

ISAIAH 54:17 MSG

COMPARISON

Each one should test their own actions.
Then they can take pride in themselves alone,
without comparing themselves to someone else.

GALATIANS 6:4 NIV

"Swipe right." If you know what that means, you know it's all about comparison. It's everywhere we look, but the perspective in which we look at things makes a huge difference.

For instance, if you had $100,000 in a third world country, you would be considered very wealthy. If you had $100,000 in a billionaire's club, that would not be the case. Sometimes, instead of enjoying the fact that we have been blessed with something good, we get lost in how it looks in comparison to others.

Why do we keep looking sideways at what everyone else is doing? If we think we're better than someone, it's sinful. If we desire what someone else has, it's still sinful. Either way, it's poor judgment.

Let's remember that God created us to be unique. He thinks that crooked tooth is cute, and He loves the way we sing out of tune. When He looks at us, He doesn't see our imperfections. If we are believers, He only sees the perfection of Jesus. Before you go to sleep tonight, think of things that make you happy being uniquely *you*! *DJ*

• • • • • • • • • •

Lord, help me be content with the way
You made me while I continue to grow
in faith and character.

Comparison is the thief of joy.

TEDDY ROOSEVELT

The Creator thinks enough of you to have sent
Someone very special so that you might have life—
abundantly, joyfully, completely, and victoriously.
God is so big He can cover the whole world
with His love, and so small
He can curl up inside your heart.

JUNE MASTERS BACHER

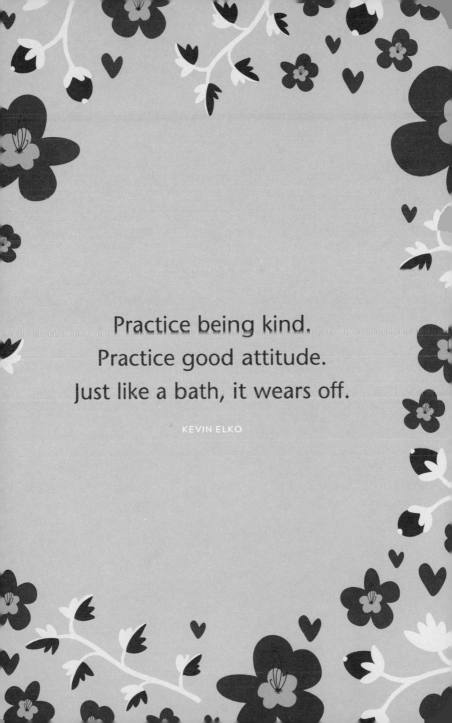

Practice being kind.
Practice good attitude.
Just like a bath, it wears off.

KEVIN ELKO

GETTING IT TOGETHER

Make me want to obey you, rather than to be rich.
Take away my foolish desires,
and let me find life by walking with you.

PSALM 119:36–37 CEV

School starts within the hour and you're still at home, running around trying to get everything you need together for the day. Pets and people clear the way as you frantically search for the last place you put your phone, keys, the project due today…even that bowl of cereal you set down somewhere. Your mind is running as fast as the rest of you as you finally head toward the door and your car. *Wait! My backpack!* you remember, and you grab it along with everything else to start your day.

Wouldn't it be great if you could just keep everything you needed for life in one simple place?

Fortunately, God gives us the best life organizer ever. It doesn't have pockets, though—just pages filled with the truth you need to keep every area of your life grounded. God's own Spirit breathed the words spoken on each page of the Bible, and they pack supernatural power when we apply them. God's wisdom and perspective give our lives one central focus—Him, providing peace as we align everything else in our lives under His sovereignty and love.

We can run ourselves crazy trying to keep up with trends and trappings everyone else says is important, or we can zero in on the one opinion that matters—God's. When His Word is our singular grounding source of truth, the rest of our life fits neatly into its proper place—surrendered to God and ready for the real world.

Today, get your game together by going to God's Word first. With your perspective lined up with His, you're ready to tackle what waits ahead! *JG*

• • • • • • • • • •

Lord, I love Your Word because it helps my scattered thoughts, and life, center calmly on You.

Recognizing who we are in Christ
and aligning our life with God's purpose
for us gives a sense of destiny....
It gives form and direction to our life.

JEAN FLEMING

VICTIM OF CIRCUMSTANCE

Give thanks in all circumstances;
for this is God's will for you in Christ Jesus.

1 THESSALONIANS 5:18 NIV

I have to admit that there are times when I don't like this verse. It's too hard. Give thanks in *all* circumstances? Even for times like when I walked into the homecoming dance with my dress tucked into my Spanx?

Then I read it more closely. It doesn't say to be thankful *for* all circumstances. It says to be thankful *in* them. To continue to praise God when we're happy, and when we're sad. When we're celebrating, and when we're broken. When it's convenient, and when it's inconvenient. When we feel thankful, and when we don't. Even when we are right smack in the middle of something awful.

It all sounds good, but how are we supposed to do something that is so against our human nature? We remember what Christ did for us. We remember what He has brought us through already. And we remember that whatever we face in the future, God's grace is bigger than our circumstances.

The next time you find yourself in the middle of a difficult situation, take a deep breath. Pause in the middle of the chaos to thank God for at least one good thing. *DJ*

• • • • • • • • • •

Lord, help me to be faithful to You at all times,
and in all circumstances.

Don't lie in the squalor of your past.
Choose to make what Jesus did *for* you
bigger than what others did *to* you.

CHRISTINE CAINE

HONESTLY

*For it is by grace you have been saved, through faith—
and this is not from yourselves, it is the gift of God—
not by works, so that no one can boast.*

EPHESIANS 2:8–9 NIV

Sitting there with her youth group, she smiled and played along. Her leader was awesome, always full of so much energy—and faith, something she secretly struggled to find for herself. If she was honest, she'd say that all the other kids just seemed more spiritual than her, though she worked hard to keep up her Christian façade. Deep down, though, she felt different—like a fraud. *Will I ever find faith that's real and works?* she worried.

If we are honest with ourselves and each other, we know we're all secretly a mess. Simple doubt or outright rebellion can lurk beneath the surface of seemingly submissive behavior, and let's face it: it isn't easy trusting a God you can't see with your eyes.

That's what makes God's invitation to us so awesome. Faith in God is a gift, not something we generate ourselves. We simply ask God for it and He gives it, starting small like a mustard seed. It grows as we walk in obedience. He is faithful to always finish the work He starts, so we don't have to worry. God will grow us up in Him as we submit to His Spirit's power that He planted in us. *JG*

. . . .

Father, thank You for giving me faith,
and by that faith I trust You to change me
into the person You made me to be.

And now, Israel, what does the Lord your God
ask of you but to fear the Lord your God,
to walk in obedience to him, to love him,
to serve the Lord your God with all your heart
and with all your soul, and to observe
the Lord's commands and decrees that
I am giving you today for your own good?

DEUTERONOMY 10:12–13 NIV

OUR HELPER

*But the Advocate, the Holy Spirit, whom the Father
will send in my name, will teach you all things
and will remind you of everything I have said to you.*

JOHN 14:26 NIV

I've been asked how God can be the Father, the Son, and the Holy Spirit at the same time. I explained it with an apple. We can think of the red exterior as God the Father. It's all around the apple, just like God is always around us. Then we have the sweet, white part that feeds us. I think of that part as Jesus. His sweet teaching feeds our hearts and minds. Deep inside are the seeds. They are unseen inside the apple, just like the Holy Spirit lives unseen inside each of us.

The apple has these three parts, but it is still one apple. God has three parts, but He is still one God.

We've seen the cartoons where the person has a little devil on one shoulder, representing what's *easy*, and a little angel on the other shoulder, representing what's *right*. Which do we listen to? If we ask God for guidance, that helper on our shoulder will be the Holy Spirit, re-minding us of everything that is good and right. If it's nourished, it will grow into something wonderful! *DJ*

. . . .

Holy Spirit, let me recognize Your voice
when You speak to my heart.

When I was little, I thought the name
Holy Spirit and Holy Ghost sounded scary.
I liked calling Him my Helper instead.
I can't see Him, but I know my Helper is there
because I can hear Him talk to my heart when
I don't know what to do. Now, if only
He would help with my homework!

JOSHUA BOWEN

BOLD TYPE

The wicked flee though no one pursues,
but the righteous are as bold as a lion.

PROVERBS 28:1 NIV

Sometimes I like to put myself in other people's shoes, especially the ones of those I admire in the Bible. I wonder, what does it take to be brave like Moses, who led the masses out of Egypt—or Joshua, who jumped into command to claim Israel's promised land? David defeated Goliath by great faith, and Daniel defied the king to stay true to God. *But how? How did they go from ordinary lives to extraordinary bravery?*

In every case, being with God birthed incredible boldness. Moses literally glowed with glory after talking with God face-to-face. Moses mentored Joshua, who often stayed behind in the tent just to get more time alone with God. David spent his youth worshipping God out alone with the sheep, and Daniel developed a reputation for his daily times alone with God in prayer.

Do you have dreams to do something great for God one day? God loves it when we do! He is a great big God who is able to do more than anything we ask or imagine. But He wants our hearts first. When we draw near to God with our full attention, He fills us with His Spirit and fuels us with a supernatural confidence to be as bold as a lion for Him. *JG*

• • • • • • • • • • •

Father, You make me brave!
Thank You for drawing near to me
when I draw near to You.

Grasp the fact that God is for you—
let this certainty make its impact on you in relation
to what you are up against at this very moment;
and you will find in thus knowing God
as your sovereign protector...both freedom
from fear and new strength for the fight.

J. I. PACKER

FAMILY MATTERS

Though my father and mother forsake me,
the Lᴏᵐᴚ will receive me.

PSALM 27:10 NIV

Families are very different. You might be a person who has all of your wants and needs taken care of by a family that loves you. You might have a divided family, where nobody gets along. Maybe you were taken away from your birth parents and live with an adopted family. Maybe your parents struggle with addiction. Maybe you have been abused. Maybe you feel like your parents are always in your business and don't trust you. Maybe you wish someone would check on you a little more.

Whatever your situation, it's a sure bet that your family will let you down at some point. Not intentionally, but it will happen. You will let them down too. We are human, and we make mistakes. This is a perfect opportunity for you to extend grace and mercy to them. You see, grace is not only meant to be received. It's also meant to be given.

What if they haven't shown grace to you? What if they don't deserve it? Well. Do we ever deserve what Jesus did for us? That's the beauty of it. Grace is a form of unconditional love. Let them see Christ in your actions. *DJ*

• • • • • • • • • •

Father, help me be able to extend grace to others,
even when it is difficult.

God does not want perfection.
He wants repentance.

DR. RAY GUARENDI

God doesn't love us because we're good.
He loves us because *He's* good.

JOYCE MEYER

IDENTITY THEFT

*Stay alert! Watch out for your great enemy, the devil.
He prowls around like a roaring lion,
looking for someone to devour. Stand firm
against him, and be strong in your faith.*

1 PETER 5:8–9 NLT

You hear about it happening all the time. Some smart but evil computer genius—maybe even in another country—hacks into your information online. Within minutes he has all the details he needs to take over your accounts, spend all your money, and ruin your credit. It's a disaster! By inadvertently giving over your identity, you lose everything.

But the situation is even worse in the spiritual realm. Believers are Satan's choice target for identity theft. He knows that every child of God is perfectly loved and provided with all of heaven's richest blessings. While he can't change our status, he can alter our perception of it. Daily he seeks to sabotage our confidence, wheedling our minds with worries and doubt. He whispers words of self-hate, buoyed by guilt and shame. And if we listen to his lies, we end up a crumpled mess.

But God is our firewall, our shield against Satan's schemes. When we choose to believe who God says we are—holy and dearly loved children—we extinguish enemy fire. Free from confusion or conflict, we rest with quiet confidence in God alone, who gives us our names and keeps us safe. *JG*

• • • • • • • • • •

Jesus, I choose to believe what
You've said in Your Word and I stand
against Satan's schemes!

Self-rejection is the greatest enemy
of the spiritual life because it contradicts
the sacred voice that calls us the "Beloved."
Being the Beloved constitutes
the core truth of our existence.

HENRI NOUWEN

BEING HUMBLE

But he gives us more grace.
That is why Scripture says:
"God opposes the proud
but shows favor to the humble."

JAMES 4:6 NIV

e've all gone out of our way to make sure we look our best. Maybe we got a new outfit, or spent a crazy amount of time applying makeup and fixing our hair just right. We do multiple checks in the mirror to be sure we aren't smiling with something stuck between our teeth. We know that nervous feeling in the pit of our stomach when we enter a room.

The common theme in all of that is we are thinking a whole lot about ourselves. There's nothing wrong with wanting to look our best, but it's important to ask ourselves why we are doing it. Are we trying to impress people with our looks, or are we trying to please God with our actions?

The next time you are getting ready to go out, and praying that nobody saw that embarrassing picture on

Snapchat, why not also pray that God shows you who might need an encouraging word? A compliment? A friend? Maybe we can help someone else get rid of that uneasy feeling in the pit of their stomach. *DJ*

• • • • • • • • • •

Father, help me to find a healthy balance
between having confidence in myself
and having too much confidence in myself.

For attractive lips, speak words of kindness.
For lovely eyes, seek out the good in people.
For a slim figure, share your food with the hungry.
For beautiful hair, let a child run his
or her fingers through it once a day.
For poise, walk with the knowledge
you'll never walk alone.

SAM LEVENSON

We have missed the full impact
of the gospel if we have not
discovered what it is to be
ourselves, loved by God,
irreplaceable in His sight,
unique among our fellow men.

BRUCE LARSON

THE POOL PROBLEM

Be very careful, then, how you live—not as unwise but as wise, making the most of every opportunity, because the days are evil. Therefore do not be foolish, but understand what the Lord's will is.

EPHESIANS 5:15–17 NIV

It's frustrating, isn't it? You're feeling alone and you just want to hang with your friends, relax, and get a little time together. So you tweet, text, message, and Snapchat to see who's free, but no one is. Everybody is too busy with school, sports, work, *whatever*. But next weekend rolls around and now you're the one with an overloaded schedule. Life just feels too crowded. Why can't we fit in everything we want?

Maybe because, like everyone else, our pool is too full. We've filled our lives with so much that we can't keep it contained, and our attention is spilling out everywhere, leaving us feeling more spread out and emptier than ever before.

Fortunately, Jesus invites us to a better way, one that works with the way we are designed. But to walk in it, we must learn how to and be willing to say "no" to some of our options. Ask God to help you weed out the time wasters and watch God direct your steps to what's best. With God's Spirit in the lead, your life will find the balance it needs. *JG*

. . . .

Jesus, please help me create
the right space in my life to keep
what's most important in place.

There is a time for everything,
and a season for every activity
under the heavens.

ECCLESIASTES 3:1 NIV

DOING WHAT'S RIGHT

The LORD is more pleased when we do what is right and just than when we offer him sacrifices.

PROVERBS 21:3 NLT

It's challenging to do what's right and take the high road sometimes, isn't it? Our family has had tough conversations about how doing the right thing is often the most difficult. When someone is mean to us or someone we love, our human side might want to seek revenge or yell at them. However, are we any better? Are we measuring our actions against God's standards or the world's standards? How do we know the difference?

A rule of thumb I have always used is that if it's the truth, it doesn't change with the whims of society. And in order to know that truth, we must study the Bible. After we know what God says in it, then we can do our best to live it.

God tells us to demonstrate the fruit of the Spirit, which is love, joy, peace, patience, kindness, goodness, gentleness, faithfulness, and self-control. We are not to demonstrate vengeance. Or post malicious words on social media. Or hold a grudge. When we do what's right and keep God as the focus instead of the disappointments, everything else will align, and we will be blessed. *DJ*

• • • • • • • • • • •

Dear Jesus, I have faith in You.
Let Your grace shine through me so I can be
the fruit of the Spirit for others.

If you have to think too long about
whether something is right or wrong,
it's usually wrong. Sometimes Satan
is just trying to talk you into something.
When you pray and talk with God,
you will know. Listen to Him.

YVONNE DAVIS

LESSONS IN LAVA

Don't be angry or furious.
Anger can lead to sin.

PSALM 37:8 CEV

On TV, you watched the images of earth exploding upwards with flaming hot lava oozing down mountains. As the molten rock flowed over trees and villages, it incinerated everything in its unfortunate path. While it might be a sight to see on your screen, it's not an experience you'd want to witness in real life.

And yet if you know an angry person (or if you are that angry person), you've experienced similar explosions of the emotional kind. One minute you think everything is fine, but one wrong word or move sends a mountain of heat your way. Where does all that fury come from, and what happened to set it off?

Whether the explosion comes from you or your friend, it's time to do a little excavating. Ask God for wisdom to see below-the-surface symptoms of anger to find whatever is feeding it. While it could be some righteous cause burning inside us, nine times out of ten it's a sin of some sort that needs to be confessed. When we keep a clean slate with God, we create room in our souls for His Spirit to pour out the right kind of words, spouting fountains of hope instead of fumes of destruction. *JG*

• • • • • • • • • •

Father, please help me control my temper
and make my words be helpful
to those who hear them.

No matter how just your words may be,
you ruin everything
when you speak with anger.

JOHN CHRYSOSTOM

FORGIVENESS

Then Peter came to Jesus and asked, "Lord, how many times shall I forgive my brother or sister who sins against me? Up to seven times?" Jesus answered, "I tell you, not seven times, but seventy-seven times."

MATTHEW 18:21–22 NIV

When we have really been hurt, sometimes we don't want to forgive. We're angry! We might even want revenge. Maybe we feel like forgiving the other person is letting them off the hook.

Forgiveness doesn't free them from the consequences, but it does free us from the anger. It's not saying that what they did was okay. It's allowing us to get rid of the bitterness in our hearts.

What if they aren't sorry? Forgive them anyway. What if they keep hurting us over and over again? That's a hard one, but forgive them anyway while distancing yourself from them. How many times do we want God to forgive us? Any great relationship is built on two great forgivers.

When you are having a difficult time forgiving some-one (even yourself!), how might things turn out differ-ently if you took it to God in prayer? *Continuously.* While you're at it, what if you prayed for the ones who need to forgive *you* as well? You might be surprised at how much a little grace can soften your heart. *DJ*

* * * * * * * * * *

Father God, remove any bitterness in my heart,
and help me be a better forgiver.

Nothing stirs God's heart more than a humble heart and a merciful spirit. God responds to mercy, because it is through compassion that we fully come to know Him. This is the defining quality of a true follower of Christ. We are never closer to the heart of God than when we are forgiving someone. And we are never farther from it than when we are holding a grudge.

NICKY CRUZ

SOUL SILENCE

He says, "Be still, and know that I am God;
I will be exalted among the nations,
I will be exalted in the earth."

PSALM 46:10 NIV

Your mom booked the appointment, and you've managed to make it on time. But now you're sitting in the dentist's lobby and you realize you left your phone at home. *Aaawesome!* you think. *I can choose between golf or parenting magazines.* What will you do?

If we're honest, we all really work hard to keep our attention occupied. Whether it's a check on our in-box or social status at the red light, or scrolling through Instagram at the table, even a minute of unused time can feel like an eternity. Our electronic addiction may actually be our hang-up to hanging out with God. Life just feels more comfortable when we keep on the go.

But God says to be still. Literally, stop moving... or chatting, or surfing, or scheming, or worrying or complaining and just get away and simply. Be. Still.

Remember that He is God.

It may take a few minutes in soul silence before we hear it, but God's whisper comes in the quiet. He invites us to breathe in the beauty of all that He is as His Spirit revives in us who we are. In the stillness we realize who and what matters most. *JG*

• • • • • • • • • •

Lord, I don't want to miss You.
Help my hurried mind to slow down
and simply be with You.

So wait before the Lord.
Wait in the stillness.
And in that stillness,
assurance will come to you.

AMY CARMICHAEL

PASSING THROUGH

So we fix our eyes not on what is seen,
but on what is unseen,
since what is seen is temporary,
but what is unseen is eternal.

2 CORINTHIANS 4:18 NIV

When we're young, it might be the coolest toy at Christmas. As teens, it might be the newest phone or a nicer car. As adults, it could be a higher-paying job or a bigger house. We never really outgrow the desire to have something better.

There is nothing wrong with having nice things. Money is not the root of all evil. The *love of money* is. We have to be sure we aren't buying things just to keep up appearances. Having the best of everything might be the dream for some, but if it is the goal for our lives here on earth, we are in trouble. We're simply passing through. Our time here is for one reason: to prepare for heaven. How are we doing that? *Are* you doing that?

Perhaps, instead of *buying* better things, we can spend more time *doing* better things. Let's make our passing through create a real difference for what is eternal. *DJ*

• • • • • • • • • •

Dear heavenly Father, when I lay my head down
at the end of each day, I pray that I can do
so knowing I grew a little closer to You
in the time You gave me.

I'm going to skip in the sunshine!
I'm going to race with the puppy!
I'm going to pick out a wedgie and
not care who's looking! God gave us this
beautiful day, and I will use it to be happy.

EMILY BOWEN

MATH TESTS

Consider it pure joy, my brothers and sisters, whenever you face trials of many kinds, because you know that the testing of your faith produces perseverance. Let perseverance finish its work so that you may be mature and complete, not lacking anything.

JAMES 1:2–4 NIV

It's like math, life is—the simple kind, like A+B=C. If you train really hard and work out, you get in shape. If you read the book and study your outline, you do well on your test. If you give your heart to God and work hard to do His will, you live a pain-free life.

Wait.

Except that pain-free thing doesn't really pan out in reality. We wish it were that easy, and sometimes we secretly strategize to make God give us the life we want by pulling all the right strings, but God's life equations factor in a lot more variables. Trials are actually one of the chief tools He uses to produce the kind of character results we can't get any other way.

When hard times come into your life (and they will), don't miscalculate God's intentions. He's not against you or trying to hurt you. As the best Father in the universe, He's arranging heaven and earth to result in your biggest blessing. Trust Him to work out the problem in His time, using your current pain to shape a more amazing future with Him. *JG*

· · · · · · · · · ·

*Father, help me to trust You during
the difficult times, that You will use them
to make me grow stronger.*

God has not promised skies always blue,
flower-strewn pathways all our lives through;
God has not promised sun without rain,
joy without sorrow, peace without pain.
But God has promised strength for the day,
rest for the labor, light for the way,
grace for the trials, help from above,
unfailing sympathy, undying love.

ANNIE JOHNSON FLINT

LOSS

Brothers and sisters, we want you to know what happens to those who die. We don't want you to mourn, as other people do. They mourn because they don't have any hope. We believe that Jesus died and rose again. When he returns, many who believe in him will have died already. We believe that God will bring them back with Jesus.

1 THESSALONIANS 4:13–14 NIRV

I have been blessed to see life come into this world. Sadly, I've also seen it go out. It's okay to be sad and grieve when we lose someone we love. Even Jesus wept when He heard of the death of His friend.

If we believe in the resurrection of Jesus Christ, our grief is mostly for ourselves. We miss our loved one terribly! At the very same time, we can also rejoice for them. Their last day here is their first day in heaven!

Time may not heal all wounds, but God can. We come to Him in our brokenness, and give Him all the pieces. My grandma used to tell me that for every "Good

Friday" of life, there is always an "Easter Sunday." How wonderful it is to know that death is not the end! It's just a new beginning. *DJ*

• • • • • • • • • •

Jesus, thank You for dying on the cross
so that we can live with You in eternity!

It's so strange how loss is so personal.
It feels like nobody in the whole world
has grieved as deeply as you have.
Yet, it's something we experience universally.
If you've gone through it and know what it's like,
reach out to someone else in their pain.
They will never forget your kindness.

HEIDI GARCIA

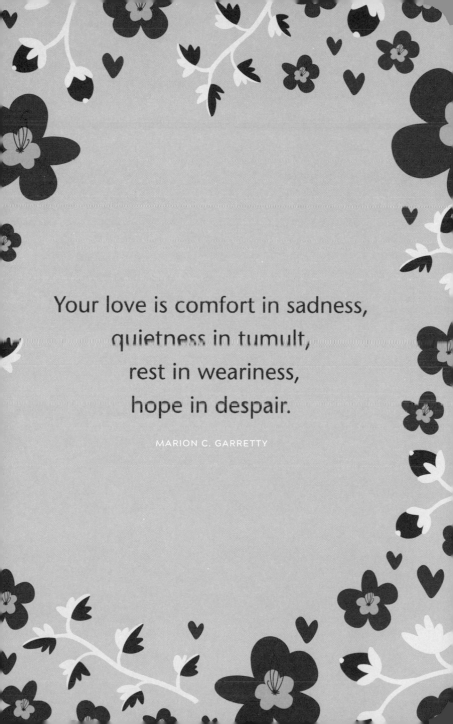

Your love is comfort in sadness,
quietness in tumult,
rest in weariness,
hope in despair.

MARION C. GARRETTY

WAKE-UP CALL

There is a friend who sticks closer than a brother.

PROVERBS 18:24 ESV

Everyone in school knew he was a player, with a whole string of heartbroken girls proving his reputation. But when she opened his message and saw his smile, she melted. *He's just soooo cute*, she thought dreamily, flattered that he'd thought of her. She flirted back with a quick message and would have fallen for his ruse if her best friend wasn't watching it all unfold. "Are you out of your mind?" she shrieked, and stole her phone away. A few minutes later, she brought her friend to her senses.

The truth is, all of us have fickle hearts. Even when our minds know what's best or right, we feel our emotions run in the opposite direction and almost everything in us wants to go with them. We need friends who not only share our faith, but who also feel comfortable calling us out when we're headed the wrong way. And we need to be that strength for them too.

Along with good friends, God also gives us His Spirit to guide us. Whenever you feel the tide of emotions pulling you where you know you don't need to go, just cry out to God for help. He's eager to give us the wisdom we need and the will to tame our errant hearts with the truth of His grace. *JG*

• • • • • • • • • •

Lord, when I let my emotions take over,
please send Your Spirit to bring me to my senses.

Friendship is the fruit gathered from
the trees planted in the rich soil of love,
and nurtured with tender care
and understanding.

ALMA L. WEIXELBAUM

YOUR CALLING

Each of you should use whatever gift you have received to serve others, as faithful stewards of God's grace in its various forms.

1 PETER 4:10 NIV

When someone asks what you are really good at, how do you answer? Maybe you can rattle off a list of things fairly easily, or maybe it takes you a few minutes to think of something. Either way, we are all given things that we are naturally good at. Each of us has strong areas that may be someone else's weakness. (And the other way around.) That way, none of us end up thinking we can do it all on our own. We need each other, as "faithful stewards of God's grace."

When we get a strong urge to use our gifts or talents for a greater good, that is when our gifts become our calling. Are you keeping your gifts and talents all to yourself, or are you using them to serve others? Maybe you can find somewhere to volunteer, or mentor someone who has interest in your talent. Ephesians 4:1 tells us to live a life worthy of the calling we have received. Since God gives each of us a calling, He will probably ask how we used it. Let's be able to give Him a wonderful answer! *DJ*

• • • • • • • • • •

Thank You, Father, for the joy
my talents bring to others!

I've experienced a cloud of witnesses
in heaven and on Earth, praising with me,
weeping with me, and watching with me
as God takes a very earthly body
and heals it for Him to be more glorified.
I continue to hold on to my post
until God raises my replacement!

LORI CONLEY

WAGING WAR

(ON THE RIGHT ENEMY)

*Put on the full armor of God, so that you can take
your stand against the devil's schemes. For our struggle
is not against flesh and blood, but against the rulers,
against the authorities, against the powers of
this dark world and against the spiritual forces
of evil in the heavenly realms.*

EPHESIANS 6:11–12 NIV

The daughter didn't say a word, but her clenched jaw and dagger-like eyes drew the battle lines. She wasn't going down without a fight, and this argument with her parents had all the ingredients for an atomic explosion. Though the fallout might hurt even her, freedom to go where and when she wanted was worth whatever price.

Sometimes it feels like a cosmic collision when our parents put the brakes on our plans. *Why do they always want to block what I want?* we wonder. It's easy to excuse their ideas as outdated and dismiss their instructions as uninformed.

We are fighting a battle for sure, but when we show disrespect and refuse to submit to our God-given authority, we *always* lose. It may feel like the whole problem is your parents, but the Bible says our fight is not against flesh and blood. We have spiritual forces all around us seeking to destroy us. Dividing families is their weapon of choice.

Even when we can't agree on an issue, we can realize who the real enemy is. Pray for help to speak honestly in love, and let God guide your plans—even through your parents. You'll avoid Satan's trap and win true freedom in the end. *JG*

Father, I will trust You to lead me through
the authority figures You have placed in my life.

Should we feel discouraged, a simple movement
of heart toward God will renew our powers.
Whatever He may demand of us, He will give us
the strength and courage that we need.

FRANCOIS FENELON

DESPERATION

In my distress I called to the LORD;
I cried to my God for help.
From his temple he heard my voice;
my cry came before him, into his ears.

PSALM 18:6 NIV

Sometimes we just feel broken. No amount of well-meaning cards or words from friends makes a difference. The loss is too great. The pain is too much. The heartache is unbearable. If one more person tell us that we'll feel better soon or that we shouldn't feel so bad, we might scream!

Well, maybe we do need to scream, but not at the people who are trying to make us feel better. Sometimes, in our brokenness, we can cry out to God. He will hear our anger, our sadness, our anguish, and our frustration. He will hear the humble desperation in our voice, and He will understand it. Remember, God knows what it's like to see His only Son suffer.

This is earth. Not heaven. Unfortunately, there will be broken moments. We can take some comfort knowing that it's okay to pray those desperate prayers that drive us to our knees. It's okay to let God see the open wounds that we're afraid to let anyone else see, and ask Him to heal our hearts. *DJ*

• • • • • • • • • •

Lord, knit together the broken pieces of my heart, and help me find joy again.

You can never learn that Christ is all you need, until Christ is all you have.

CORRIE TEN BOOM

You keep track of all my sorrows.
You have collected all my tears in your bottle.
You have recorded each one in your book.

PSALM 56:8 NLT

IN PROCESS

*Being confident of this, that he who began
a good work in you will carry it on to completion
until the day of Christ Jesus.*

PHILIPPIANS 1:6 NIV

When the youngest sister burst into tears, the three older sisters groaned almost simultaneously. "Why does she have to be so dramatic about eeevvvverything?" the eighteen-year-old asked (quite dramatically). They had already forgotten how much support and encouragement *they* required at her age to just keep going.

Without people to encourage and believe in us—even when we're struggling—we all wilt, no matter what age we are. God put us into community, and especially into families, where we can build a strong network of support when we seek to love each other consistently, through the good and ugly moments.

The truth is, growth is struggle in process. It means stretching and learning, leaving and leaning—and yes, failing and succeeding. If we want to mature emotionally and spiritually as we grow up, we need to give ourselves and others room to develop. Instead of demanding perfection from ourselves or our friends and family, we find tremendous rest and peace when we create space for grace. Understand that God is at work, and none of us are finished yet! In fact, our mess-ups actually make the best teachers.

We are all *in process* of reaching the full potential God places in each one of us. Our job is to encourage others and ourselves to keep on trying, trusting God to cause the growth we want to see. *JG*

· · · · · · · · · ·

Father, please fill me with Your Spirit as I patiently
wait for You to work in me and my family.

A wise gardener plants her seeds, then has
the good sense not to dig them up every few days
to see if a crop is on the way. Likewise,
we must be patient as God brings the answers…
in His own good time.

QUIN SHERRER

THANK GOD!

*Always giving thanks to God the Father for everything,
in the name of our Lord Jesus Christ.*

EPHESIANS 5:20 NIV

Have you ever wanted something so badly that you found yourself negotiating with God? We go to Him in prayer, and hear ourselves saying that if He would just do this one thing for us, we would do something for Him in return. We ask as if God needs something from us. (He doesn't.) If we are going to do something for God, we should be doing it because our hearts want to honor Him, and not because we feel like we have to keep up our end of some deal we created.

Instead of negotiation, what if we thanked God *ahead of time*? Before that dream becomes a reality. Before we go to that interview. Before we have that difficult discussion with someone we love. Before we take that test. Before we do something we are afraid to do, why not thank God in advance for what we know—in faith—He will answer for us?

Keep in mind that God isn't a genie in a bottle who grants wishes upon request. And just like any good father, sometimes His answer is no. But when His timing aligns with our plan, wonderful things can happen! *DJ*

• • • • • • • • • •

Thank You, Father, for prayers
that have yet to be answered!

Thanksgiving—
always precedes the miracle.

ANN VOSKAMP

I am so beyond thankful for my family, friends,
and friends like family. And I'm thankful that
God gave us one another to carry out
what He put in our hearts to do.

SARA MANNING

THE REAL DEAL

We will not be influenced when people try to trick us with lies so clever they sound like truth.

EPHESIANS 4:14 NLT

As she walked into the clothing store, she couldn't keep her eyes off the life-sized photos lining the wall. Every one depicted a beautiful (and of course, skinny) girl with some gorgeous guy, laughing and living up the good life. The room itself smelled like romance—and rich living. Mesmerized by every incoming sensation, she decided, *I want that! Why can't that be me?*

The marketing worked because she asked the wrong question. Had she asked how real was the relationship portrayed in the pictures, she might have thought differently. The photos were of fake lives put there to sell overpriced clothes. If she had first considered how much more she could get for her money in some other store, she'd could have missed the tantalizing marketing entirely—marketing that made her feel bad about herself, like she was less than others.

Our culture clamors for instant gratification, promising prosperity and romance if we just buy in: *Why wait? You, too, can get what you want right now!* But in the compromising transaction, we're left with only broken promises and fake images of intimacy.

If we want the real deal, we must leave the world's empty pictures of success behind and believe God instead. Wait on God to give you what's best at the right time, and enjoy authentic relationship with Him all along the way. *JG*

• • • • • • • • • •

Father, I don't want to be fooled
by what the world says. My hope—
and my eyes—are fixed on You.

God desires authentic dialogue.
As we speak what is on our hearts,
we are sharing real information that
God is deeply interested in.

RICHARD J. FOSTER

CHOOSE JOY

*Consider it pure joy, my brothers and sisters,
whenever you face trials of many kinds,
because you know that the testing
of your faith produces perseverance.*

JAMES 1:2–3 NIV

Okay, wait a minute. Is God asking us to be happy that we have trials to go through? Well, not exactly. This verse is asking us to look for joy. You see, happiness and joy aren't the same. Happiness is a feeling that changes with our mood. If I'm happy that it's sunny outside and then it starts raining, I might not feel happy anymore. Joy is a choice. Joy is what we choose when we are right smack-dab in the middle of the unhappiness. If it's raining in the middle of my sunny day, I can choose to look for rainbows!

When you're having a horrible day, but focus on something positive...
When you look to God for hope in a hopeless situation...

When you spread encouraging words rather
than gossip…
When you sing when your heart feels like
crying…
When you pray before you react…
When you forgive the hurt…
…you choose joy!

James is teaching us that when we're going through trials, we have a choice. We can feel defeated and sorry for ourselves, or we can let our faith be greater and choose to persevere in spite of the trials. We can choose joy! *DJ*

• • • • • • • • • •

*Jesus, I will lay my trials at the foot of the cross
and watch Your joy grow in my faithfulness.*

If you do whatever Mom says, her life is a lot
happier. And if you do it the first time,
your life is a lot happier.

BENJAMIN BOWEN

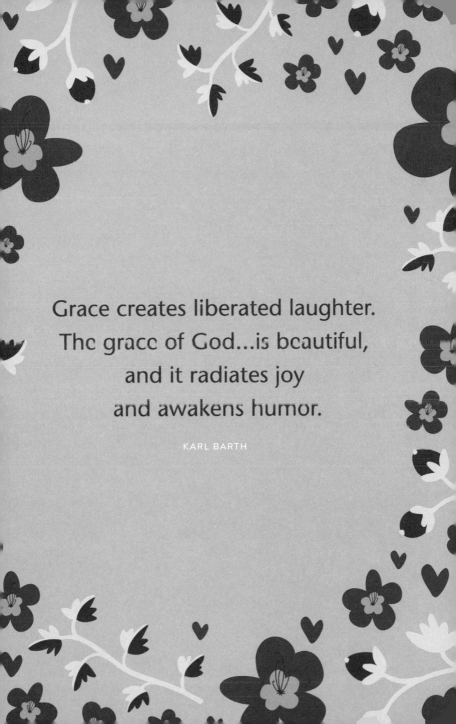

Grace creates liberated laughter.
The grace of God...is beautiful,
and it radiates joy
and awakens humor.

KARL BARTH

THE BEST WAY TO WALK

The Lord has told you what is good.
He has told you what he wants from you:
Do what is right to other people. Love being kind
to others. And live humbly, trusting your God.

MICAH 6:8 ICB

Just weeks ago, she first tried standing, pushing her legs straight from the crawling position. Steadied by the coffee table's edge, the infant-turning-toddler saw where she wanted to go. *But how to get there?* She teetered between the table and freedom. Both parents coaxed her forward, arms extended just beyond reach of her own.

One step forward. Then she fell.

But it was a start! Within the month, she mastered her wobbly legs and began to walk with confidence.

And so it is with all God's kids. No matter what age we are when we first place our faith in Christ, we all start off as spiritual infants. We nourish our newborn faith with simple truth from God's Word. But that's only the start. God intends for us to grow...to stretch our legs as we step out in obedient faith!

Like the toddler, we learn to walk with God one step at a time. We move one step closer to maturity every time we remember God's Word, ask for His help, and obey what we learn. Moment by moment, decision by decision, our ability to move with God's power improves. In time, we'll be walking on steady legs, eyes fixed on our Father with outstretched arms. *JG*

* * * * * * * * * *

Jesus, I don't want to just know
what's right; I want to do it.
Please give me strength to follow You.

As we grow in our capacities to see and enjoy
the joys that God has placed in our lives,
life becomes a glorious experience
of discovering His endless wonders.

DENIAL

*If anyone is ashamed of me and my words in this
adulterous and sinful generation, the Son of Man
will be ashamed of them when he comes
in his Father's glory with the holy angels.*

MARK 8:38 NIV

Have you ever been ridiculed for your faith? Have you ever felt ashamed to admit that you are a believer when everyone else is not? If so, you're not alone. That happened to Peter, one of the closest friends and disciples of Jesus. In John 18, we read about how Peter denied Jesus three times on the day He was crucified.

Some think Peter did this out of fear that he would also be scourged. Others think he was simply embarrassed. What we know for sure is that when Peter realized what he had done, he was so ashamed!

In John 20, we see how Peter was the first to race into the empty tomb of Jesus, and he dedicated the rest of his life to bring others to believe.

If we ever catch ourselves in a similar situation, I hope we also race to our Lord! We can ask the Holy Spirit to give us the perfect words to stand up for what we believe. Our words might be a great witness for someone else! *DJ*

• • • • • • • • • •

Lord, give me Your strength,
so that I always stand firm in my faith.

When you stand, God will contend
with those who contend with you.
The truth always outlasts a lie.

LISA BEVERE

CASTING CROWNS

Christ himself was like God in everything.
He was equal with God. But he did not think that
being equal with God was something to be held on to.
He gave up his place with God and made himself
nothing. He was born as a man and became
like a servant. And when he was living as a man,
he humbled himself and was fully obedient to God.
He obeyed even when that caused his death—
death on a cross. So God raised Christ
to the highest place. God made the name
of Christ greater than every other name.

PHILIPPIANS 2:6–9 ICB

The announcer called her name, and she was elated. A smile bigger than Texas stretched across her face as she strode across the stage to claim her crown, as the winner of the pageant. But just when they placed it on her head, a commotion broke out among the judges. Within seconds, the mistake was made public. They had announced the wrong queen! And now, she had to hand over the crown.

Can you imagine the humiliation? Once we're declared the winner—in anything—we never want to cede our position.

That's what makes what Jesus did so extraordinary. Though King of kings and Lord of lords, Jesus lowered Himself on purpose, exchanging His royal crown to wear the rags of our humanity. When He should have been seated in the highest place of honor, Jesus our Lord chose to serve sinners instead.

He led the way to a new kind of beauty—the crowning glory of a servant's heart. Though the world will fail to see His worth, let us keep in step by following His lead. God's path to glory begins with humility. Lower yourself to serve others as Jesus did, and God will lift you up in the right time. *JG*

* * * * * * * * * * *

Jesus, I don't understand why You gave up
everything for me, but I am forever thankful.
Help me to love and serve like You.

In your lives you must think
and act like Christ Jesus.

PHILIPPIANS 2:5 ICB

LEAVING A LEGACY

I am reminded of your sincere faith,
which first lived in your grandmother Lois
and in your mother Eunice and,
I am persuaded, now lives in you also.

2 TIMOTHY 1:5 NIV

There's a church high on a hill in Cincinnati. Every Good Friday for over a century, thousands of people from many faiths have gathered to "pray the steps" that stretch from the Ohio River up to that church. My great-grandparents were among the many who would pray and reflect on what a great gift Christ gave us.

Eventually, my grandmother took her own children, and then my mother took my sisters and me. It's probably not a surprise that I take my own family every year I can. We have stood in long lines, and in blistering sun. We have prayed through cold rain, and in the dark. We have prayed when we were rejoicing, and when we were grieving. It hasn't always been easy, but it was always worth it. Praying the steps has become a family tradition. Living with sincere faith has become our legacy.

It's a blessing to be surrounded by faithful people. If you don't have that, know that *you* can be the one who begins a long line of sincere faith in your family. Begin today! *DJ*

· · · · · · · · · ·

Dear Jesus, may all the generations
praise You and adore You.
Let me be Your light in mine!

If it's too small to pray about,
it's too small to worry about.

WILMA FORREST

DEPENDENCE DAY

Some trust in chariots, others in horses.
*But we trust the L*ORD *our God.*

PSALM 20:7 NIV

As night descended, the crowd of onlookers gathered around, pulling up lawn chairs and blankets to best view the show. Vibrant red, green, gold, and blue fireworks burst with a heart-thumping bang and filled the dark sky with colors and sounds of celebration—our nation's way of remembering when we first won our independence.

As young adults with college or work just around the corner, we've anticipated an Independence Day of our own. Since we first learned to tie our shoes to now managing much more adult issues, we've been preparing ourselves for that moment when we leave home to handle life on our own. Isn't independence what we're all working toward?

Not if you're a believer! While externally we're learning how to be an adult, inwardly God wants our child-like faith to grow. Instead of becoming more independent in our thinking, He wants us to learn deeper dependence on Him. As we learn to lean on Him more and more in our daily decisions, the hard work of growing up in the real world gets less daunting. Though we grow to stand on our own two feet, we're clinging firmly to our Father. Every day with God, we celebrate Dependence Day with Him! *JG*

· · · · · · · · · ·

Lord, I can't do anything of worth without You.
I depend on You alone for my strength and life.

But blessed is the one who trusts in the LORD,
whose confidence is in him. They will be like
a tree planted by the water that sends out
its roots by the stream. It does not fear
when heat comes; its leaves are always green.
It has no worries in a year of drought
and never fails to bear fruit.

JEREMIAH 17:7–8 NIV

CASTING STONES

*Let any one of you who is without sin
be the first to throw a stone at her.*

JOHN 8:7 NIV

One day the Pharisees brought a woman to Jesus who had been accused of committing adultery. The punishment for such a crime was to be stoned to death. When they asked Jesus what they should do, He basically told them they could publicly accuse her of her sin if they had never sinned themselves. In other words, don't be hypocrites.

If we're being honest with ourselves, aren't we all a little hypocritical at times? We've all sinned. Yet sometimes we still participate in gossip. Or share someone's embarrassing picture. Or tell someone's secret. Yes, sometimes we are the ones casting stones.

After the Pharisees considered what Jesus said, they dropped their stones and walked away. Afterward, Jesus addressed the woman face-to-face:

"Woman, where are they? Has no one
    condemned you?"
"No one, sir," she said.
"Then neither do I condemn you," Jesus declared.
    "Go now and leave your life of sin."
    (John 8:10-11 NIV)

Yes, there was a consequence for her sin. However, instead of condemning her, Jesus showed an entire community what grace looks like. When we find ourselves with stones in our hands, how can we do the same? *DJ*

• • • • • • • • • •

Father, help me put my stone down
and show others what grace looks like.

Grace is greater than your sin. Grace is greater than your past mistakes, your secrets, your failures. It's greater than whatever addiction you've battled or abuse you've suffered. Whatever you can fill in that blank, grace is greater than that.

KYLE IDLEMAN

There is a difference between
grace and mercy.
Mercy is the decision of God
not to punish us.
But grace is the decision of God
to save and bless us.

MAX LUCADO

DREAM BIGGER

*Now to him who is able to do immeasurably
more than all we ask or imagine,
according to his power that is at work within us,
to him be glory in the church and in Christ Jesus
throughout all generations, for ever and ever! Amen.*

EPHESIANS 3:20–21 NIV

"We have a surprise for you today." The parents gently nudged their sleeping children awake. "You need to get up and get ready." Stretching and yawning, they began guessing.

"Are we going to the park?" Nope.

"The zoo?" Not that either.

"Think bigger!" the parents challenged. By now both kids were sitting up. "The pool?"

The parents could hold back no longer. "Disney World! We're spending the week with Mickey!"

Can you imagine the excitement? The kids just couldn't conceive of that level of fun, though their parents had every detail already planned.

We're a lot like that. We belong to a God whose power and creativity is limitless. Before we were even born, He planned the perfect adventure for our lives, a calling that not only draws us closer to our Creator, but also allows us to play a pivotal role in His kingdom work. He planned our personality, giftings, and environment to set the stage. And now it's time for us to wake up and realize the potential that lies before us!

Don't settle for small-town thinking. Ask God to help you dream bigger as He works His incredibly awesome plan in and through you! *JG*

• • • • • • • • • •

God, open my eyes to Your greatness and give me
a vision for how I can best serve You.

The goodness of God is infinitely
more wonderful than we will ever
be able to comprehend.

A.W. TOZER

EAR CANDY

Praise him with tambourine and dance;
praise him with strings and pipe!
Praise him with sounding cymbals;
praise him with loud clashing cymbals!
Let everything that has breath praise the Lord!

PSALM 150:4–6 ESV

One of my favorite things to do is to crank up some good tunes in the car and sing. Loudly. It's not uncommon in my house to turn on the music and have a spontaneous dance party. Dancing and singing is so much fun! It can lift our spirits, relieve stress, make us laugh, and bring so much joy.

There are times, though, when a song comes on with a really great beat, but really bad lyrics. Maybe it's popular and fun, but when I weigh it against what God would want me to hear, I know I should probably flip the station.

Just like the books we read, the words we say, and the movies we watch, once something unholy goes into our minds, it's there. It's emblazoned on our brains to be replayed at any given moment. It works both ways, though! We can just as easily fill our minds with things that praise God. How pleased He must be when the images and lyrics that come to mind are ones that bring us closer to Him! *DJ*

• • • • • • • • • •

Thank You, God, for the gift of music!
Let me use it to praise Your name.

I'm so grateful that God has allowed His heart
for people to translate through music,
to impact the lives of so many,
just like a loving Father would.

LAUREN DAIGLE

IDOL THOUGHTS

Fear the L<small>ORD</small> your God, serve him only
and take your oaths in his name.
Do not follow other gods, the gods of the peoples
around you; for the L<small>ORD</small> your God,
who is among you, is a jealous God.

DEUTERONOMY 6:13–15 NIV

It was *so* hard to relating to Japan's foreign culture. Down every city and rural street, she saw shrines of various kinds. People placed trinkets inside to appease whatever idol or ancestor they worshipped there. *Why would anyone worship man-made objects that have no power to hear or help?* she wondered.

And then God's Spirit spoke to her heart. *Where do you go looking for hope, and how do you spend your time?*

Immediately, she thought about her friends—and how she sought their advice first before God. And then she thought about her phone. How much time did she spend on a screen instead of Scripture? And boys? She didn't even want to think about all the wasted energy there.

Suddenly foreign cultures didn't seem quite so crazy. We all have the tendency to worship false idols.

But God calls us higher. He is jealous for our affection and attention, telling us to put *nothing* before Him in our time, talents, thoughts, and choices. We were all made to worship; our soul is intentionally designed with a God-shaped vacuum inside. Something will fill it. Will we choose whatever passing pleasure or empty promise the world provides, or will we worship the only One who fills and heals the hole in our souls? *JG*

• • • • • • • • • •

Lord God, nothing is more important than You.
Teach me to turn away from worthless things.

Lord, my strength and my fortress,
my refuge in time of distress, to you the nations
will come from the ends of the earth and say,
"Our ancestors possessed nothing but false gods,
worthless idols that did them no good."

JEREMIAH 16:19 NIV

TEMPTATION

*No temptation has overtaken you except
what is common to mankind. And God is faithful;
he will not let you be tempted beyond
what you can bear. But when you are tempted,
he will also provide a way out
so that you can endure it.*

1 CORINTHIANS 10:13 NIV

I t's been said that someone once asked Billy Graham how he had managed to avoid scandal during all the years he spent away from home and in the public eye. He replied that God will never allow us to be tempted without giving a way of escape.

See, Mr. Graham was not saying that temptation never happened. However, when it did happen, he knew that if he relied on God, the temptation would not be so strong that he couldn't find a way to avoid it.

Satan is a masterful tempter. He knows our human weaknesses and finds a way to twist them around until a lie seems justified in our minds and looks like truth. Sometimes it's difficult to recognize which is which.

When we find ourselves struggling with temptation, how much different might the outcome be if we pause before we act? Instead of relying on our own emotion, what if we look for the way out God provides? *Then take it! DJ*

• • • • • • • • • •

Dear God, open my eyes to see the way
out of the lies that tempt me.

When your power ends, God's power
is only beginning. When you are weak,
that is when He is strong in you!

VICTORIA OSTEEN

Right is right, even if everyone is against it.
Wrong is wrong, even if everyone is for it.

WILLIAM PENN

X-RAY VISION

*He gives wisdom to the wise and knowledge
to those who have understanding; he reveals deep
and hidden things; he knows what is in the darkness,
and the light dwells with him.*

DANIEL 2:21–22 ESV

Finally, it all made sense—the ache in her wrist, her loss of strength, and the shooting pains in her arm when she exerted pressure. Finally, she asked her mom to take her to the doctor. And with one simple x-ray, the girl knew: she had a greenstick fracture—a bone so slightly broken you can barely see it, yet the source of all her pain and problems. A simple cast would cure it.

X-rays are awesome for seeing below the surface. Don't you wish we had something like that to see into our souls, too? We all live with aches and pains that show up in surface symptoms like depression or anxiety, anger or bitterness, even though we often can't trace the source.

But we know the One who can. God sees deeper into our hearts than any machine ever could. Most amazing of all, He still loves us despite what lurks there. He wants our healing process to begin, but we must visit the Healer first.

Is there something nagging at you that needs mending? Or do you have a friend who seems to be suffering? Ask God, who reveals our secret wounds and is kind enough to heal them with His power and love. *JG*

* * * * * * * * * *

*Father, search every part of my soul
and show me where I need to be healed.*

God's fingers can touch nothing
but to mold it into loveliness.

GEORGE MACDONALD

IMPOSTORS

He was a murderer from the beginning,
not holding to the truth, for there is no truth in him.
When he lies, he speaks his native language,
for he is a liar and the father of lies.

JOHN 8:44 NIV

When we hear something enough, we can start to believe it, even if we know in our heart that it's not true. People around us might have us convinced that we are not smart enough, or pretty enough, or thin enough. Or maybe we hear the exact opposite. We might hear that we are the perfect student, or the perfect child, or the perfect friend so often that we no longer see the flaws in ourselves.

People sometimes say that a "little white lie" won't hurt anyone. Or what other people don't know won't hurt them. Well, maybe. Unless it does.

John tells us that lying is Satan's native language. He is a deceiver and wants us to believe his lies. Don't fall for it, friends! John goes on to say in 14:6 that Jesus is "the way and the truth and the life." Trust in Jesus. He is the light that will speak truth in the midst of darkness, show grace in the midst of shame, and bring us out of the lies that weigh us down. *DJ*

•   •   •   •   •   •   •   •   •   •   •

Thank You, Jesus, for Your powerful
truth and light.

Make no mistake: Satan's specialty
is psychological warfare.
If he can turn us on God ("It's not fair!"),
or turn us on others ("It's their fault!"),
or turn us on ourselves ("I'm so stupid!"),
we won't turn on him. If we keep fighting
within ourselves and losing our own
inner battles, we'll never have
the strength to stand up and fight
our true enemy.

BETH MOORE

Without the grace of Jesus:
a hopeless end.
With the grace of Jesus:
an endless hope.

RICK WARREN